# Consecutive Exposition

## A Weighing of Iain H. Murray's "Time for Caution"

Tim J. R. Trumper

# DEDICATION

In grateful remembrance of John Calvin (1509–64), consecutive expositor *par excellence*, to mark the 450th anniversary of his death.

He being dead yet speaks.

# CONTENTS

Acknowledgments  vii

1  Introduction  1

2  What Is Welcome?  8

3  What Is Weak?  20

4  Conclusion  48

# ACKNOWLEDGMENTS

It is only fitting in an analysis of the homiletic comment of Rev. Iain Murray, cofounder of The Banner of Truth Trust, that I set my comments in a longer and broader context of gratitude and indebtedness.

What a blessing I and my undergraduate friends received in the late 1980s as the student offer of Banner books came to hand each year. We were by no means alone as young Christian adults in starting our personal theological libraries through the generous help of the Trust. Besides lapping up many a publisher's Foreword, presumably written in the main by Mr. Murray, we inevitably came across his books. These figured among those of formative influence on my thinking, feeling, and decision-making during those years, and thereafter as a student for the ministry. I especially recall his historical discussion of eschatology in *The Puritan Hope* (1971), his biography of Jonathan Edwards (1988), and his two-volume series on the life of Dr. Martyn Lloyd-Jones (1982 and 1990). These were read for both information and inspiration. I never came away disappointed even when, over time, I began forming my own views in response to what was gleaned from Mr. Murray's writings.

Leaving Wales in 1989 to study for the ministry at the Free Church of Scotland College (now Edinburgh Theological Seminary), I met Mr. Murray and was privileged to enjoy hospitality kindly prepared by Mrs. Murray. This was supplemented by Mr. Murray's generous and profitable gift of a two-volume set of James Bannerman's *The Church of Christ*. I have treasured it to the present, both for the memory of the evening and for the fact that the set had belonged to Jack Cullum, who founded The Banner of Truth Trust with Mr. Murray on July 22, 1957.

In time, my training for the ministry ended, but not before sensing the Lord's leading to go on and undertake doctoral studies at New College, the Divinity Faculty of Edinburgh University. I understood, even when applying, that this decision would not be universally popular among family and friends, for Mr. Murray's completion of the biography of Martyn Lloyd-Jones had injected fresh emphasis and urgency into the conservative Reformed view of the necessity of preaching. With this rejuvenated view of the primacy of preaching I concurred, but did not see then, nor do I see now, a necessary conflict between preaching and doctoral research.

In summer 1993 following graduation from the Free Church College, I completed a summer internship at Grove Chapel in Camberwell, London. With two weeks to go prior to the commencement of the doctoral research, I received a phone call from Mr. Murray passionately encouraging me to enter into the ministry rather than to take up the doctoral work. This was not an unwarranted intervention on his part, but a response to his receiving a check to co-sign from Mr. Austin of London who had generously promised to fund the research. Naturally, I lauded Mr. Murray's concern, and can still hear his voice from that conversation in my mind. He sufficiently cared for the state of pulpit preaching in the United Kingdom to try and direct a young man in his ways. He was not alone. My father, Dr. Peter Trumper, and the late Rev. Omri Jenkins, erstwhile director of the European Missionary Fellowship, were also "on my heels," so to speak. In fact, as the research went on, the latter two would tease me sporadically, "Haven't you finished that doctorate yet?" To which I would reply with a grin, "No, because I've been so busy out preaching!" It was true, and gladly so. But the advice Mr. Murray had shared during that Saturday morning phone call in August 1993 has remained with me to the present, and has been put to good use with "wannabe" doctoral students more times than I can recall: "If you are going to proceed with the research, make sure your dissertation builds up the church and does not simply debate a matter for the sake of it." My prayer is that the final product, "An Historical Study of the Doctrine of Adoption in the Calvinistic

Tradition" (2001) met the criteria. I certainly intended it to.

This is all to say a big "thank you" to Mr. Murray for his influence on my thought and aspirations. My undiminished gratitude for the stimulus he has provided over the years means that I have not differed with his caution about consecutive exposition lightly, nor have I gone into print to deny or reverse my opinion of the use God has made of him. But I do feel that in the narrowing of conservative Reformed circles a party line has too often developed which encourages the reading of approved authors, but not necessarily the rigor of thought which is prepared to view matters independently if persuaded by Scripture. Whereas a tradition of theology, expressed by subordinate standards which vary modestly among themselves and allow for alternative opinions on certain issues, can embrace independence of thought, party lines, based more on friendships and reactions, struggle with what is or sounds at variance from the mode of thought and speech in vogue within the tribal context. Doubtless, the following defense of consecutive exposition may, in weighing Mr. Murray's caution, be deemed by those who understandably regard his voice as authoritative to have transgressed an unspoken party line; yet the defense is well within accepted views and practices of the Reformed tradition. When the example of Calvin's preaching is taken into account, it could be said that the defense takes us back beyond the comparatively recent example of Charles Haddon Spurgeon (1834–92)—understandably a favorite of Mr. Murray, and beloved by so many (including myself)—to the origins of the Protestant Reformation.

Accordingly, I pray that Mr. Murray will receive my response as a compliment, for not only is his caution worth an analysis, it demonstrates for his encouragement that I not only read Banner of Truth literature in my formative years, but was taught to think by the theology and concern for the church it espouses. I remain committed as ever to Reformed theology, and have not abandoned the Trust's literary output, but hope today's conservative Reformed circles can invest not only in encouraging an emerging generation to read the Reformed works now available, but to process them in the context of ministry in today's world.

This is what I have attempted here in relation to the theme of expository preaching. Not for the first time a study of mine began as an article intended for a theological journal, but burst the bounds of all acceptable word lengths. This history explains the proliferation of footnotes in my books. Yet, the inclusion of them, deemed once in friendly fashion as "footnote disease," is not something over which I lose sleep! I like to include the sort of detail, background, and qualification of argument for which I look in the books of others. It is your choice as to the degree to which you include them in your reading. All I ask is that reviewers take note of them in the cause of thoroughness and fair-mindedness.

In bringing this short study to print I am, as usual these days, indebted to friend and congregant Marilyn Van Dyke for her generous, thorough, and fun-filled editorial assistance. My gratitude is also due those of our church family and radio audience who encourage the weekly exposition of the Word. Specifically, I thank valued colleagues in the consistory and the staff who, in varying ways, do much to support the preparation of the pulpit ministry. Special thanks go in this regard to Tammy Cunningham, church secretary, and to Rev. Tom VandenHeuvel, Minister of Visitation. Most of all, I am indebted to Brenda Trumper. Her loving aid as both my wife and secretary to the pastoral staff and elders, cannot be adequately put into words. The Lord will reward her more than I ever could!

Meanwhile, it goes without saying that I bear sole responsibility for the views expressed hereafter, and for the decision to publish them. I have been stirred to share my views by a passion for the proclamation of God's revealed counsel, and trust that those who weekly expound it may gain encouragement to keep on keeping on.

Tim J. R. Trumper
Seventh Reformed Church
Grand Rapids, Michigan
www.7thref.org
www.fromhisfullness.com

September, 2014

# 1 INTRODUCTION

> The household of God urgently needs
> faithful stewards who will dispense to it
> systematically the whole Word of God, not
> the New Testament only, but the Old as
> well, not the best-known texts only, but also
> the less-known, not just the passages which
> favour the preacher's particular prejudices,
> but those which do not!
>
> John Stott, *The Preacher's Portrait*

In 2010 Rev. Iain H. Murray, an elder statesman in global Reformed circles, published some cautionary comments about expository preaching, specifically about an exclusive diet of systematic or consecutive exposition.[1] His caution has now been republished in America in the on-line *Aquila Report*.[2] By reason of its brevity, authorship, and usefulness, the caution is worth quoting in full:

---

[1] *The Banner of Truth Magazine* (557:9), 2010, and http://banneroftruth.org/us/resources/articles/2010/expository-preaching-time-for-caution/, accessed, May 19, 2014.

[2] Go to http://theaquilareport.com/expository-preaching-time-for-caution/, accessed May 19, 2014.

In a number of circles today 'expository preaching' is in vogue, and it is being urged on preachers as the way to preach. If this means that the preacher's one business is to confine himself to the text of Scripture, and to make the sense plain to others, there is nothing more to discuss; who can disagree save those who do not know that the Bible is the Word of God. But 'expository preaching' has often come to mean something more. The phrase is popularly used to describe preaching which consecutively takes a congregation through a passage, or book of Scripture, week by week. This procedure is compared with the method of preaching on individual texts that may have no direct connection with each other from one Sunday to the next. The latter is discouraged in favour of the 'expository' method.

Why has this view of 'expository preaching' become comparatively popular? There are several reasons. First, it is believed that the practice will raise the standard of preaching. By a consecutive treatment of a book of Scripture, it is said, the preacher is taken away from any hobby-horses, and congregations are more likely to be given a broader, more intelligent, grasp of all Scripture. The preacher is also delivered from a constant search for texts – he and the people know what is before them. These reasons are perhaps confirmed for younger preachers by the fact that at our main conventions and conferences the well-known speakers commonly deal with one passage in a few addresses, and when these find their way into print they are taken as models of the best way of preaching. Published sermons of any other kind are few and far between for publishers definitely favour the 'expository' on the grounds of their popularity.

## DISADVANTAGES CONSIDERED

In our view, however, it is time that the disadvantages of this view of preaching are at least considered:

### 1. Know your gifts

It assumes that all preachers are capable of making effective sermons along these lines. But men have different gifts. Spurgeon was not unfamiliar with 'expository preaching' (listening to sermons in his youth he had sometimes wished the Hebrews had kept their epistle to themselves!), and he decided it was not best suited to his gifts. There is reason to think that being an effective 'expository' preacher is not such a common gift as some seem to think. Even Dr Lloyd-Jones was twenty years into his ministry before he slowly introduced 'expository' series.

## 2. What is preaching?

The argument that the 'expository' method is the best means to cover most of the Bible is too largely connected with the idea that the foremost purpose of preaching is to convey as much as possible of the Bible. But that idea needs to be challenged. Preaching needs to be much more than an agency of instruction. It needs to strike, awaken, and arouse men and women so that they themselves become bright Christians and daily students of Scripture. If the preacher conceives his work primarily in terms of giving instruction, rather than of giving stimulus, the sermon, in most hands, very easily becomes a sort of weekly 'class' – an end in itself. But true preaching needs to ignite an on-going process.

## 3. Sermon or lecture?

Significantly, the churches – particularly in Scotland – once distinguished between 'the sermon' and 'the lecture'. The word 'lecture' was not used in any pejorative sense, it simply meant what is now commonly meant by 'expository preaching', namely, the consecutive treatment of a passage or book. The commentaries of John Brown of Broughton Place, Edinburgh, originated in this way. So did Lloyd-Jones' work on Romans – he called those expositions 'lectures'; the difference between a sermon and a lecture, in his view, being that a sermon is a rounded whole, a distinct message, complete in itself, whereas the lecture on Scripture is part of something larger and on-going. In contrast with his Romans series, Lloyd-Jones conceived the contents of his Ephesians series as 'sermons', and anyone comparing his procedure in these two series (the first delivered on a Friday night, the second on a Sunday morning), can quickly see the difference. This is not to devalue his Romans series; the purpose was simply different.

## 4. What helps the hearer most is best

At the end of the day, the best preaching is that which helps the hearers most, and in that connection the track record of the consecutive 'expository' method is not impressive. It has never proved popular in the long term, and the reason for that, I think, is clear: a sermon needs a text as the basis for a memorable message. The text may be remembered when all else is gone in the mind of the hearer. Sometimes, it is true, a text may be a paragraph rather than a verse – a Gospel parable or a narrative, for instance – but if, as often happens with 'expository preaching', a series of verses is regularly made 'the text', then a whole series of ideas get into the sermon and, clear over-all lessons (such as one may see in Spurgeon's sermons) are lost. The preacher has become only a commentator. Sometimes he even ceases to give out a text from the passage he intends to take. People could easily get the same help, and perhaps better, by taking up a book teaching the same section of Scripture.

But, it may be said, 'Is not Lloyd-Jones' Ephesians both expository and textual preaching? He enforces only a few leading thoughts at one time, and yet proceeds consecutively – why cannot others do the same?' The answer is that Lloyd-Jones did bring the textual and the expository together in his Ephesians sermons but this is exactly the type of preaching that is not within the gift of most preachers. Too many tyros have tried to preach verse-by-verse through major books of Scripture with near-disastrous results. It is arguable that this is one of the reasons why 'reformed' preaching has, in more than one place, been criticised as 'heavy' or plain 'dull'. The less ambitious, who also adopt the 'expository' mode, make no attempt to use single verses for their texts and that is the danger that too easily turns preaching into a running commentary.

5. The best 'fit' for evangelistic preaching

Evangelistic preaching does not best fit the 'expository' mode; in fact, where the 'expository' is exclusively used, true evangelistic preaching to heart and conscience commonly disappears. It may be said, that if that is true it is the fault of the man, not the passage, for is not all Scripture given by inspiration of God and profitable? Surely, it is objected, all Scripture may be used of the Spirit of God to awaken and reach the lost? It may, but it is clear from Scripture that there are particular truths most adapted to speak to non-Christians (witness our Lord's example) and that it is these truths, and the texts that best epitomise them, which have special and regular prominence in most effective evangelistic ministries. The men most used in the conversion of sinners in the past have known what these texts are – Whitefield, M'Cheyne, Spurgeon, Lloyd-Jones, and a host of others knew. Today there is some danger of their being forgotten. When did you last hear a sermon on 'What shall it profit a man if he gain the whole world and lose his own soul?'

This is not an argument that the whole concept of consecutive preaching through a passage is wrong, simply that it must not be allowed to have an exclusive place in pulpit ministry. Let each preacher find what he is best able to do, and let it be ever remembered that, whatever the method of presenting the truth, it is men filled with faith and the Holy Spirit who are needed most at this hour. More than correct teaching is needed: we need messages that will move congregations and even sway communities.

## THE TESTIMONY OF R. B. KUIPER

Lest anyone should think the above observations are novel, I close with the opinion of one of the greatest preachers of the last century, R. B. Kuiper. His biographer points out that he refused to allow the term 'expository' to be applied only to sermons given in serial form on passages or books of Scripture. The word should apply to all exposition of Scripture worthy of the name. He continues:

> It follows that it is a serious error to recommend expository preaching as one of several legitimate methods. Nor is it at all satisfactory, after the manner of many conservatives, to extol the expository method as the best. All preaching must be expository...He was also objecting to the commonly held opinion that only a running commentary on an extended portion of Scripture (a chapter, perhaps) could be called expository preaching. The running commentary type of preaching has certain glaring faults, according to Kuiper. The exegesis tends to be superficial, since so much material has to be covered. And such sermons often lack unity, so that the hearer has no clear idea as to just what the sermon is about.

Whatever method the preacher adopts, the following words of Kuiper are relevant for all:

> A simple and conversational yet forceful delivery commands both respect and response. Enthusiasm inspires. Logic is convincing, the illogical confusing. As preachers, let us have a heart. Let us stop wearying our audiences. Let us make our preaching so absorbingly interesting that even the children would rather listen to us than draw pictures and will thus put to shame their paper-and-pencil-supplying parents. But we may as well make up our minds that an absolute prerequisite of such preaching is the most painstaking preparation.

As someone indebted personally to Mr. Murray, his writings, and to The Banner of Truth Trust, and engaged in consecutive exposition which goes from our church family to radio listeners across Western Michigan, I am, like others no doubt, unable to ignore this caution. In weighing it carefully I note four points Mr. Murray makes which compel analysis:

> Firstly, that expository preaching need mean nothing more than making plain the sense of Scripture to others.

> Secondly, that the consecutive or systematic exposition in vogue in certain circles has come to be understood as the exclusive method of expository preaching.

> Thirdly, it is men filled with faith and the Holy Spirit and not the specific method of exposition who move congregations and sway communities.

> Fourthly, while consecutive exposition is not wrong, each minister of the Word must find what he is best able to do.

Now, in principle there is nothing here to dispute. In fact, there is plenty in Mr. Murray's brief comments to ponder and to take to heart. His long-standing interest in the history and quality of preaching is inspiring, as is his belief that Spirit-filled preaching is vital to the health and growth of the church today. Why then does his shot across the expositor's bow stir mixed emotions? To answer this question we analyze Mr. Murray's caution by posing two subsidiary questions: What is welcome about it? And, what is weak? I answer these respectfully, but out of empathy for the many colleagues in pulpit ministry who have more "skin in the game" than Mr. Murray, and for the sake of our hearers who need to know why we preach God's Word the way we do.

## 2  WHAT IS WELCOME?

> It is men filled with faith and the Holy Spirit
> who are needed most at this hour. More than
> correct teaching is needed: We need messages
> that will move congregations and even sway
> communities.
>
> Iain H. Murray, "Expository Preaching—Time
> for Caution"

While Mr. Murray rightly disclaims the novelty of his arguments, it is important to demonstrate familiarity with them. In summary, he states that:

1. *The exposition of Scripture does not always require a series, let alone a series through a book.*

If expository preaching "means," says Mr. Murray, "that the preacher's one business is to confine himself to the text of Scripture, and to make the sense plain to others, there is nothing more to discuss; who can disagree save those who do not know that the Bible is the Word of God. But 'expository preaching' has often come to mean something more. The phrase is popularly used to describe preaching which consecutively takes a congregation through a passage, or book of Scripture, week by week." He would have us distinguish, then, the style of exposition from the principle of it.

Mr. Murray has a point. Listen, for example, to the Westminster Assembly's *Directory for the Public Worship of God* from the section "Of the Preaching of the Word": "Ordinarily, the subject of his [the minister's] sermon is to be some text of Scripture, holding forth some principle or head of religion, or suitable to some special occasion emergent; *or* [my italics] he may go on in some chapter, psalm, or book of the holy scripture, as he shall see fit." Charles Bridges makes the same distinction, labeling the preaching of disconnected texts as "topical" and of connected portions as "expository."[3] In today's world, however, these labels are a little confusing, for they each bespeak expository preaching. Whether the preaching is "topical" or "expository" the preacher discerns the mind of the Spirit in the text and lays open its view of truth. The latter type differs only in the fact that the process continues from one passage to the next.

Obviously, then, it is exegesis and not the sequence, system, or consecutive character of the sermons that is fundamental to expository preaching. In effect, there is agreement that exposition is the *esse* of preaching, even if others of us argue that a regular diet of consecutive exposition (understood and executed maturely) is, in the pastoral context, its *bene esse*.

2. *The systematic or consecutive exposition of Scripture possesses solid benefits.*

Iain Murray lists some of them—the pursuit of a higher standard of preaching; the prevention of the minister riding off on hobby horses; the impartation of a broader, more intelligent grasp of all Scripture; and the freeing up of the minister from the constant search for a text. John Stott adds to these four benefits the way consecutive exposition eliminates the oversight or willful neglect of certain passages, and precludes the hearer from suspecting that the choice of passage is driven by individual pastoral concerns ("Who is he pointing at today?").[4] Clint Arnold of Talbot School of Theology

---

[3] Charles Bridges, *The Christian Ministry with an Inquiry into the Causes of its Inefficiency*, first published 1830 (London: The Banner of Truth Trust, 1967), 284f.

[4] John R. W. Stott, *I Believe in Preaching* (London *et al.*: Hodder and Stoughton, 1982), 315ff. For more from Stott see his *The Preacher's Portrait: Great Word Pictures*

notes a further four benefits: consecutive exposition is the best way to provide the sheep with a balanced diet, it is application oriented, models how Scripture should be read in context, and has a long history with great impact.[5] We may add another—an eleventh. In closely following the contours of Scripture—reflecting in the process its teaching, priorities, and tenor—consecutive exposition not only teaches congregants the meaning of Biblical passages in sequence, it equips them to read Scripture for themselves and to minister the message of the Bible to others (cf. Eph 4:12).[6]

In summary, we may say that "the normalization of expository preaching"—to utilize the language of one of our core values at Seventh Reformed Church—provides a Bible-based alternative to preaching that is doctrinaire (e.g. catechetical) or anecdotal (popularist).[7] Undoubtedly, Mr. Murray is familiar with these arguments, but we thank him for mentioning at least some of them.

3. *There are different levels and kinds of gifting among those called to preach.*

Given, says Spurgeon, that "no preaching will last so long, or build up a church so well, as the expository,"[8] it is necessary that the capability of expositing the Scriptures should be evident as part of a pastoral call. How the exposition takes place will obviously depend on the particular gifting of the preacher and the context and capacities of the people. In this sense, systematic expositors may agree with Iain Murray about the diversity of gifts within the call to

---

*from the New Testament*, originally published 1961; reprint ed. (Leicester, England: Inter-Varsity Press, 1995), 22–25.

[5] Clint Arnold, "7 Reasons in Support of Consecutive Exposition of Scripture" (http://thegoodbookblog.com/2011/sep/07/7-reasons-in-support-of-consecutive-exposition-of-/, accessed, May 19, 2014).

[6] Unless otherwise stated, the version of the Bible cited is the English Standard Version.

[7] http://7thref.org/ecclesial-core-values/, accessed May 19, 2014. Bridges' very fulsome itemization of the pluses of consecutive exposition covers much of what is said here (*The Christian Ministry*, 284–85).

[8] C. H. Spurgeon, *An All-Round Ministry: Addresses to Ministers and Students*, first published 1900 (Edinburgh and Carlisle, PA: The Banner of Truth Trust, 1986), 36.

preach, while seeking to enlarge their own capacities and those of their hearers in the handling of God's Word. In other words, context and capacities do matter to the expositor, but only if the acceding to these two Cs does not empower laziness or disinterest in Scripture in either the preacher or his congregants.

Given the numerous pluses of systematic exposition, we might wonder in contexts where the method is both possible and appropriate, why preachers would not want to hone their homiletic gifts by means of more systematic exposition. If, as the late J. Douglas MacMillan (1933–91) taught us at the Free Church of Scotland College, ninety percent of our hearers will not rise higher than we do in the things of the faith, why, we may ask, should our hearers have the zest to master the length and breadth of Scripture in any orderly fashion if we as preachers deem it insufficiently important to reveal from the pulpit a coherent sense of its background, shape, and scope. In Bridges's words, "A failure of bringing forth the fundamental doctrines from such resources, will prove, not the exhausted state of the treasure, but the want of spiritual and accurate observation of its hidden store."[9] Learning how to expound inscripturated revelation systematically is one way we can grow as handlers of Scripture, and enhance the Biblical grasp of our people as we do so.

*4. Preaching is more than a process of imparting information.*

Writes Mr. Murray, "It is men filled with faith and the Holy Spirit who are needed most at this hour. More than correct teaching is needed: We need messages that will move congregations and even sway communities." Since he does not identify the circles practicing consecutive exposition which elicited his cautionary note, we cannot ascertain specifically why he should think the method of preaching to work against striking, awaking, and arousing hearers, to use his words. There's nothing in the method to render the disjunction inevitable, or to say that Spurgeon's distinction between the expository and hortatory method of preaching is necessary.[10] Regardless, we heartily embrace Iain Murray's general sentiment

---

[9] Bridges, *The Christian Ministry*, 284.
[10] Spurgeon, *An All-Round Ministry*, 36.

about the need for revival, even though there's a mixture of thoughts about the way he understands it.[11] Still, he is correct to say that a homiletic method or correct teaching alone cannot determine the outcome of pulpit ministry. Understandably, then, Mr. Murray points as evidence of this to those who knew considerable unction and liberty of the Spirit. We shall question how Mr. Murray uses his heroes, but not his intent to encourage our rejoicing in how God used them, or to inspire our yearning for what Lloyd-Jones described as "Logic on fire! Eloquent reason!"[12] In fact, Lloyd-Jones's definition of preaching expresses succinctly the systematic expositor's conviction about his homiletic method and need of the Spirit's filling for the sanctification and empowerment of his efforts.

*5. The expository method can be distorted.*

Regrettably, this is true. Mr. Murray mentions some of the ways the method can become distorted, but I offer here a broader perspective on today's differing *historic-/systematic-theological, Biblical-theological, expository,* and *anecdotal* approaches to exposition.

---

[11] Strangely, Mr. Murray's exegesis and hermeneutics of revival and his espousal of its principles are dissatisfying and satisfying in equal measure. His view of the Spirit's ministry under the old covenant, at Pentecost, and in the life of the believer requires much more nuancing, even though many of Mr. Murray's historical observations very helpfully distinguish revival from revivalism (*Pentecost Today? The Biblical Basis for Understanding Revival* [Edinburgh and Carlisle, PA: The Banner of Truth Trust, 1998]). Likewise, the acceptance of Lloyd-Jones's well-documented views on the ministry of the Spirit has been hampered by his reliance on the descriptive rather than the didactic passages of the New Testament. Not only has his approach muddled the terminology of revival, it has led to a hybrid of thought in which the principled cautions against the abuse of revival are theologically Reformed but predicated on a Charismatic-like confusion of the baptism and fullness of the Spirit.

[12] D. Martyn Lloyd-Jones, *Preaching and Preachers* (Grand Rapids, MI: Zondervan, 1972), 97. We may ponder whether Lloyd-Jones's definition was influenced by descriptions of the ministry of the Southern Presbyterian James H. Thornwell (1812–62). Consider those by Northern Presbyterian J. W. Alexander, son of Archibald Alexander of Princeton, and Thornwell's biographer Southern Presbyterian B. M. Palmer, in B. M. Palmer, *The Life and Letter of James Henley Thornwell D.D., LI.D.,* first published 1875, reprint ed. (Edinburgh and Carlisle, PA: The Banner of Truth Trust, 1986), 300, and Douglas F. Kelly, *Preachers with Power: Four Stalwarts of the South,* (Edinburgh and Carlisle, PA: The Banner of Truth Trust, 1992), 61–83.

To start with, there's the *historic-/systematic-theological* approach of the continental Reformed tradition. Refreshingly, Donald Macleod asks, "Should we preach on catechisms or confessions as such? Only in the most exceptional of circumstances," he opines.[13] By mingling his arguments with the ones I have used in ending the practice of catechetical preaching at the church I serve, we can number three main reasons (inclusive of an array of subsidiary arguments) for not structuring the preaching schedule around the Heidelberg Catechism or any other subordinate standard.[14]

Firstly, there is the obvious point that Scripture is solely authoritative for faith and conduct. The nomenclature "subordinate standards" is in this sense a misnomer. They have no authority outside of the Word, and can be legitimately used for so long and so far as they concur with Scripture (cf. Belgic Confession Arts. 5 and 7; Westminster Confession of Faith 1:4). Rightly does Macleod say: "Our mandate is to preach the Word. To resort instead to expounding a human document is to confuse our people by blurring the distinction between what is normative revelation and what is to be judged by that revelation." The very fact that those steeped in catechetical preaching struggle to go without the use of the catechism demonstrates the point.

Secondly, the Bible is the fully revealed counsel of God. This has several implications for preaching. Think of its *context*. The doctrine of Scripture is set against the backdrop of redemptive history and the organic unfolding of revelation. Although creeds and

---

[13] Donald Macleod, "Preaching and Systematic Theology," in *The Preacher and Preaching: Reviving the Art in the Twentieth Century*, edited by Samuel T. Logan Jr. (Philipsburg, NJ: P&R, 1986), 269.

[14] My main arguments against the use of the Heidelberg Catechism for the structuring of the preaching were summarized in the March 2012 issue of *The Voice*, the magazine of Seventh Reformed Church. We seek to retain attention to these heads of doctrine in the youth Sunday School program and in district studies, and believe the discussion format offers an opportunity to embed the teaching more deeply in the minds of attendees. While it is true that this approach does not catch everyone in the church family, it is also true that most of those not attending Sunday School or a district study would be insufficiently interested to take in much from a catechetical sermon or to run with what they hear in order to follow up with self-education.

confessions can and do provide some redemptive-historical context, there's nothing like returning, in vintage Reformed fashion, to the fount of our doctrine (*ad fontes*). Additionally, God's revealed counsel determines the *scope* of preaching. To let the Heidelberg Catechism, with its limited coverage of Scripture, dictate the schedule of preaching, even if at just one end of the day, is to withhold from hearers seismic tracts of Scripture and the opportunity to hear the pulpit discussion of multiple issues. Furthermore, God's counsel determines the *content* of preaching. We are not, says Macleod, to swap the "proportion, balance, and selection of topics" of what God has revealed in his Word under the extraordinary operation of the Spirit (which is his allotment for his glory and our needs) for the apportionment of human wisdom operating under the ordinary influence of the Spirit. What is more, God's revelation determines the *media* of Scripture. In it we have a multi-genre library, in the Heidelberg Catechism a uni-genre document. There is divine wisdom in the former, for the preached Word has different types of hearer. If a person struggles to perceive the truth through one genre he or she can receive it better through another. The options are plentiful: history, poetry, proverbs, letters (whether didactic, practical, or both), and apocalyptic. The tapestry of Scripture is rich and cannot be served well by a dogmatic construal which enlists seemingly related texts to unpack a theme irrespective of their contexts, authorial diversity, and figures of speech. I argue not that the classic subordinate standards are unbiblical or that the Christian church should not make use of subordinate standards—far from it!—but that the adoption of the practice of preaching Scripture through a subordinate standard constituted a reform of the church which went too far, notwithstanding the weight which is placed on catechetical preaching for conveying the chief heads of doctrine.

Thirdly, Macleod reminds us that "confessions and catechisms present doctrine abstracted from its existential context—the life-situation of Scripture—and thus obscure its practical relevance or tempt us not to apply it at all." This argument, applied to issues of personal salvation and piety, is more relevant to Presbyterians than to the continental Reformed, given the differences in feel between the Westminster Standards and the Heidelberg Catechism. That said, Presbyterians do not go in for catechetical preaching. Applied to missions, it must be said that the Scriptures recognize the more cosmopolitan world in which we live far more than do the Eurocentric subordinate standards of the sixteenth and seventeenth century. To see what I mean, consult the World Reformed Fellowship's 2011 Statement of Faith. Note its truly global representation of contributors and issues addressed.[15]

This is all to say that the otherwise worthy call for doctrinal preaching is not to be confused with the doctrinaire preaching of the catechetical method. Whereas doctrinaire preaching preaches Scripture through the Heidelberg Catechism (typically), doctrinal preaching only permits the subordinate standard entrance into preaching through Scripture. In other words, the exposition of a Biblical passage may be suitably illustrated from subordinate standards, but it is not the creed, confession, or catechism which drives or even construes the exposition. Whereas the Biblical theology of Scripture (the redemptive-historical portions plus the remainder) is essential to the expository method, the systematic theology of the subordinate standard is essential for the catechetical counterpart. The former is fitting for worship, the latter for a Sunday School class or a class on theology.

More briefly, there's the *Biblical-theological* approach which over-applies the otherwise happy emergence of Reformed Biblical theology. Although an advocate of the injection of greater Biblical-theological considerations into the discipline of systematic theology, it seems to me that redemptive-historical preaching is Biblical theology on homiletic overload. This point is reached when the historical narratives of Scripture are utilized to the neglect of the nonhistorical, and the great acts of God in Christ are accented to the detriment of practical application. It is, then, expository preaching well done, with its embrace of all genres and uses of Scripture, which is the authentic homiletic expression of the emergence of Reformed Biblical theology. "The Scriptures," Edmund Clowney writes, "are full of moral instruction and ethical exhortation, but the ground and motivation of all is found in the mercy of Jesus Christ. We are to preach all the riches of Scripture, but unless the center holds all the

---

[15] http://wrfnet.org/about/statement-of-faith#.U5HSK_mwL0c, accessed June 6, 2014.

bits and pieces of our pulpit counseling, of our thundering at social sins, of our positive or negative thinking—all fly off into the Sunday morning air."[16] Redemptive-historical preaching does not capture, then, the breadth of Scripture, nor the balance of Calvin, who was both the consecutive expositor *par excellence* and the most Vosian before Geerhardus Vos.

Since Mr. Murray's caution takes issue in reality against the abuse of the *expository* approach, we ought not to spare the method some scrutiny. Doubtless, the reputation of true consecutive exposition has been harmed not only by redemptive-historical preaching but by those who many would take to be true expositors but who operate by means of the Bible commentary method. This confusion Mr. Murray attributes to the publication of conference series, for publishers favor expository sermons on the ground of their popularity with readers. But it is not clear to me that conference speakers have, traditionally, been any more guilty of the Bible commentary method than Sunday preachers. What has become problematic is the regular Sunday worship in which local pastors, influenced by their published heroes (many of whom went into print near or following retirement from pastoral ministry), deem the printing of their sermons the way to ape them. Instead, therefore, of arduously transposing their sermons into chapters after the fact, they sped up the process by turning up to preach with chapter in hand. The sermon thus became for such preachers little more than the attesting of the draft chapter. Congregants became in turn but unwitting spectators of a literary refinement process. In the substitution of the primacy of preaching for the primacy of publication, the dominant thrust of the sermon went missing. While kindness precludes the provision of plentiful examples of this contemporary practice, it is nevertheless true to say that consecutive exposition has, in the hands of such a preacher, become confused with the Bible commentary method Iain Murray rightly laments. Rarely do preachers ask each other these days "What are you preaching on currently?" They are as likely to ask "What writing projects are you working on?"!

---

[16] Edmund P. Clowney, "Preaching Christ from all the Scriptures," in *The Preacher and Preaching*, 191.

In a context like this there is a need to embrace once more the glory and primacy of true exposition and the earnestness of homiletic delivery. Not only does such multitasking affect the art of preaching, it disrespects congregants, reducing them to spectators of a literary refinement process. It is worth remembering that the Jesus we preach was a preacher, not an author (Mark 1:38). He never wrote a book. I am not saying that preachers cannot be authors, but when we ascend the pulpit steps with chapters in our hands, it is time to contemplate whether we still believe preaching to be, along with prayer, the primary focus of our calling.

More briefly yet, we may refer to the *anecdotal* approach which retains connection to exposition by means of Biblical and theological sound bites, but in reality has forsaken a substantive interaction with the text of Scripture. Mr. Murray does not address anecdotal preaching any more than he does the catechetical method, but Peter Jensen does in a way worth quoting:

> We live in a time when considerable thought should be given to what constitutes "biblical" preaching. Despite protestations to the contrary, there is a manifest failure of confidence in the Bible among evangelicals. Their sermons have a biblical appearance, with references to texts and stories from the Bible, but the truth of the matter is that anecdotes and quotations take the place of exposition as the substance of what is said. Such preaching acts as a barrier between the listener and the Scripture, preventing the congregation from reading the Bible except in the most superficial way. Admittedly, expository preaching which actually puts the hearer in touch with the passage is difficult. Initially, it is not as interesting as anecdotal preaching. In the end, however, it both creates and satisfies a deep and serious hunger for God's word and a thoroughgoing impatience with human-centered, clever, and entertaining pulpit oratory. In the end, too, it is the only way to proclaim the transcendence and glory of God. Mere sermons on God will not achieve this important goal—we must allow Scripture to teach the truth in its own way.[17]

---

[17] Peter F. Jensen, "A Vision for Preachers," in *Doing Theology for the People of God: Studies in Honour of J. I. Packer*, edited by Donald Lewis and Alister McGrath (Leicester, England: Apollos, 1996), 219–20.

So, yes, exposition has indeed been distorted—more than Mr. Murray indicates, and by those not practicing it, as well as by those purporting to. Systematic expositors of God's Word, who endeavor to expound Scripture with sensitivity to the text, lament this most of all.

### 6. *Soul-winning is truly important.*

Rightly and most fittingly, Rev. Murray keeps before us, with Spurgeonic and Lloyd-Jonesian emphasis, the importance of preaching evangelistically. Evidently, he agrees with Jesus that the Scriptures speak supremely of him (John 5:39). He is also keen in effect for ministers of the Word to "do the work of an evangelist" (2 Tim 4:5). This means we must preach the big gospel texts. Although the point seems self-evident, Mr. Murray fears these are not preached on enough in consecutive exposition, and when they are they become lost in the shuffling through the verse-by-verse exposition. As a result, such gospel texts lose something of their brilliance of color and of hope.

Now those who love most of all to preach evangelistically (whether from individual sermons or amid consecutive exposition), don't want to see these fears transpire either. But the problem is not methodological, it is spiritual. We need to ensure that the love of Christ and of those he came to save come before a love of the text. This I learned from Rev. Alex MacDonald of Buccleuch and Greyfriars Free Church of Scotland, Edinburgh, who confessed that he gave up consecutive exposition because he felt he was preaching the text rather than preaching Christ.[18] While neither the preaching of individual texts nor the big gospel texts guarantees better results, or that the salvation of souls is the sole criteria for assessing a ministry, we who consecutively expound the Scripture can nevertheless keep before us Mr. Murray's challenge and that of Spurgeon, one of his heroes:

---

[18] Recently Rev. MacDonald retired. His reflections on his ministry in the Free Church of Scotland are found at http://www.freechurch.org/index.php/scotland/news_events_item/rev_alex_macdonald_retires/, accessed May 28, 2014.

Brethren, mark those who woo sinners to Jesus, find out their secret, and never rest till you obtain the same power. If you find the very simple and homely, yet if you see them really useful, say to yourself, 'That method will do for me;' but if, on the other hand, you listen to a preacher who is much admired, and on enquiry you find that no souls are savingly converted under his ministry, say to yourself, 'This style is not the thing for me, for I am not seeking to be great, but to be really useful.'[19]

Whether souls won is *the* criterion for assessing preaching is a matter for discussion, but we may certainly concur with the need to heighten its profile in Reformed preaching today.

---

[19] Spurgeon, *An All-Round Ministry*, 43–44.

# 3  WHAT IS WEAK?

As the history of preaching is unfolded, it becomes clear how important the orderly, systematic preaching through the scriptures has been a favorite system of preaching over the centuries. One is surprised to discover how many of history's great preachers made a regular practice of preaching through one book of the Bible after another.

Hughes Oliphant Old, endorsement of *The Lectio Continua Expository Commentary Series*

For all this common ground, there are plenty of factors which preclude the principled consecutive expositor from relinquishing his approach to pulpit ministry. Consider the following:

1. *The manner of argumentation.*

Although Mr. Murray's caution is brief, its implications are many and varied—hence in part the length of this analysis. However, the caution contains a number of surprising infelicities.

Firstly, we observe that Mr. Murray knocks down a straw man. When he warns that systematic or consecutive exposition must not be allowed an exclusive place in pulpit ministry, we ask, "When was it ever?" There may be isolated pockets of our Reformed world where no highlights of the Christian calendar exist—no acknowledgement of Christmas, Easter, Ascension, or Pentecost; no additional recognition of Mother's or Father's Day either, and where consecutive exposition continues its onward march through baptismal and communion services, such that the method truly is exclusive. But, if such pockets exist, they are very small and are not the ones Mr. Murray refers to as "in vogue."

Even those of us dedicated to preaching the Scriptures consecutively take breaks for different occasions. Note that Charles Bridges gets this: "The *expository* scheme . . . by a judicious mixture with the topical system [the exposition of disconnected texts], forms a most important vehicle of instruction."[20] We leave off series which go beyond certain numbers of sermons in a row (my practice is ten or fifteen and even these may be broken up), and for the sorts of events just mentioned. By the time both the capacity of our hearers and the disruptions of the calendar are taken into account, the expositor needs to press forward, for a series needs a certain momentum to carry along the congregation. We would prefer, then, to work to improve our series than to swap consecutive exposition for the regular diet of disconnected texts. These lack overall purpose or goal. In Douglas Kelly's words: "Something of the divine logic does seem to be lost when the preacher fails to work through an entire book, for the more expository method will generally be better informed by the very sequence and connection of one passage, doctrine and thought with another which follows."[21] Beside, a regular diet of disconnected texts cannot guarantee what Mr. Murray seeks from consecutive exposition, namely, Spirit-filled application.

Secondly, Mr. Murray is less than even-handed in formulating his caution. Generally speaking, it is hardly fair to compare some ministries which were exceptionally blessed without the use of consecutive exposition with examples in his mind which constitute in reality either the abuse of consecutive exposition or sequential exposition poorly executed. Now, no one questions the fact that there have been great servants of God who have preached other than

---

[20] Bridges, *The Christian Ministry*, 284.
[21] Kelly, *Preachers with Power*, 165.

by means of consecutive exposition, for after all God is sovereign in whom he uses, and as to how and when he uses them. Dr. Lloyd-Jones reminded us of this, if I recall aright from my reading, that God's sovereignty can clearly be seen in the way he greatly blessed the Arminian ministry of John Wesley. But this does not mean to say that consecutive exposition is wrong (a point Mr. Murray concedes), or that consecutive expositors have gone without God's great blessing (the examples of which Mr. Murray plays down or omits [see below]).

Consider more specifically the use Mr. Murray makes of his heroes.[22] Here we see the want of evenhandedness to work in two ways. On the one hand, he makes much of Spurgeon who eschewed consecutive exposition. His citing of Spurgeon's youthful wishing that the Hebrews had kept their epistle to themselves is unconvincing, and is possibly unjust to the expositor in view since we have no recording of him (Prov 18:13, 17). It is one thing for Mr. Murray graciously to cover the failings of his heroes, but another to quote them with approval. Spurgeon was not infallible; he was young when he made the assessment and may simply have been reflecting the fact that consecutive exposition was not his gift. Regardless, is it ever right to wish, however wittily, that a portion of Holy Scripture had been lost to history? What was meant to reflect on the expositor actually reflects on the Scripture or on our attitude toward it.

On the other hand, there is the even less convincing use of Lloyd-Jones's ministry to undercut the value of consecutive exposition. Mr. Murray attempts this in different ways. First, he points to the length of time it took Lloyd-Jones to slowly introduce expository series. This is understandable. After all, he changed vocations without retraining—a fact Mr. Murray omits from consideration. It is worth contemplating, by comparison, how long it would take before we preachers could perform a surgery if we swapped professions without retraining! The fact of the matter is that Lloyd-Jones introduced the preaching of series and to great effect. Acknowledging this, Mr. Murray next seeks to argue the variety of

---

[22] For an understanding and defense of Mr. Murray's notion of hero—the person of "spiritual, Christian greatness"—see his volume *Heroes* (Edinburgh and Carlisle, PA: The Banner of Truth Trust, 2009), ix–xiii.

Lloyd-Jones's expositions, distinguishing his connection of the text and exposition on the one hand, and the Friday night Romans series and the Sunday Ephesians series on the other. Not all, however, would agree. Tony Sargent writes: "It is difficult to draw any major, consistent differences between his [M Ll-J's] Romans' and Ephesians' series in terms of type, even though the latter were preached on Sunday mornings, the occasion he dedicated to preaching experientially". [23] Thirdly, Mr. Murray plays on the uniqueness of Dr. Lloyd-Jones. While it is understandable that an older generation who saw Lloyd-Jones at the height of his power and influence should remain affected by God's use of him, is it really the case that you need to be a Lloyd-Jones to pull off consecutive exposition? Frankly, this borders on hero worship. It is one thing to wisely counsel young preachers not to attempt too much too soon, but quite another to dissuade them from learning the craft. All to say, there is more middle ground than Mr. Murray acknowledges between the remarkably capable and the incapable. At the end of the day, the reputation of the ascended Christ who gave gifts to the church is impacted by Mr. Murray's somewhat elitest view. Our Christ gives more gifts than we know, and our Helper more empowerment than we realize. We step forward in faith to expound the Word not because we think we are "the Doctor," but because God provides for every generation and does not allow his Word to return to him empty (Isa 55:11).

In short, Mr. Murray's caution would have carried more weight had he compared his two heroes: Spurgeon and Lloyd-Jones. But would he then have been able to caution us to the same extent?

### 2. *The omission of Scripture.*

Curiously, we hear from Mr. Murray about Holy Writ, and of famous preachers of God's Word—Whitefield, McCheyne, Spurgeon, and Lloyd-Jones, of course—but nothing *from* Scripture. This is in line

---

[23] Tony Sargent, *The Sacred Anointing: The Preaching of Dr. Martyn Lloyd-Jones* (Wheaton, IL: Crossway Books, 1994), 255–56. Cf. Gaius Davies' recollections of Lloyd-Jones's expositions of Philippians, 1 John, and his more evangelistic evening series in "Physician, Preacher, and Politician: Dr. D. Martyn Lloyd-Jones (1899–1981)," in *Genius, Grief, and Grace: A Doctor Looks at Suffering and Success*, expanded edition (Fearn, Ross-shire: Christian Focus Publications, 2001), 354.

with trends within the conservative Reformed world, in which there is the danger of history becoming the rival of Scripture as the touchstone of our faith and conduct. "We are laboring for eternity," Spurgeon reminds us, "and we count not our work by each day's advance, as men measure theirs; it is God's work, and must be measured by His standard."[24]

Now although "consecutive exposition" or "systematic exposition" is not found therein, any more than are the terms "trinity," "providence," or "sacrament," Scripture is nevertheless our guide. While, says Jay Adams, "The principal biblical words translated 'preaching' do not correspond exactly to that activity to which we affix the label,"[25] we may nevertheless note certain texts which are programmatic for understanding our task.[26] They speak to:

*a. The scope of preaching:* Consecutive exposition is based on Paul's premise that "All Scripture [*pasa graphē*] is breathed out by God and profitable" (2 Tim 3:16). While equally inspired, Scripture is, admittedly, unequally important and profitable. Nonetheless, its profitability is as extensive as its inspiration and is to determine what we preach. We expound not just the great gospel texts, the ones the minister favors, or those the people like to hear, but all of it, at least in representative fashion.

The systematic expositor finds it much easier to keep track of how he's doing in this regard than the preacher offering the diet of individual texts. Take, for instance, the ministry of Dr. Geoff Thomas. After forty-plus years in Alfred Place Baptist Church, Aberystwyth, he can tell you how much of Scripture he has preached. The last I heard, he had preached all sixty-six books minus four (with some preached more than once). Not only can he approach God humbly in life and in death and report that he's preached the sacred Word, he can, more likely than not, claim to have done so in a better balance than the preacher of random texts. Others, remaining in their congregations for a briefer tenure, can attest to the same.

---

[24] Spurgeon, *An All-Round Ministry*, 18.

[25] Jay E. Adams, *Preaching with Purpose: The Urgent Task of Homiletics* (Grand Rapids, MI: Ministry Resources Library [Zondervan], 1982), 5.

[26] For more thorough ways lying beyond the scope of this essay, see Stott, *The Preacher's Portrait, op. cit.*

Commencing at Seventh Reformed Church in 2007, I set out to preach series that would cover "all Scripture" so that in the event of being called away I could be satisfied in having done that, although on a more selective scale. By God's grace we've completed seven books of the Bible (including Acts) plus sizable bites of the Law, the Prophets, and the Writings, the Gospels, the epistles, and the apocalypse. While there is always room for improvement in the quality of the expositions, and for growth in learning the needs of the people, it is at least possible to begin entering into the apostle Paul's testimony to the Ephesian elders that he had not shrunk back from preaching the whole counsel of God (Acts 20:27). Preaching "all Scripture" methodically is the route to such confidence.

*b. The use of Scripture:* Consecutive exposition of all Scripture reflects the entire gamut of its uses. Scripture is profitable, continues Paul in 2 Tim 3:16, "for teaching, for reproof, for correction, and for training in righteousness." According to Adams, the first of these terms, *didaskalia*, is closest to our modern word for preaching (cf. 1 Cor 4:17; 1 Tim 4:16, 5:17), but includes *paraklesis* (aid, assistance, advice, exhortation, encouragement, and urging), *paramutha* (comfort, cheer), and *nouthesia* (counsel, admonition). On this understanding, we need not apologize for the essential didactic role of consecutive exposition. Interestingly, Paul does not mention the use of Scripture for evangelism, but given that true *didaskalia* in pulpit ministry is never divorced from the gospel, we're likely best to understand gospel content and application to run through all the uses of Scripture (cf. 2 Tim 4:5); for although the *ekklesia* are the called-out ones, their assemblies are open. Accordingly, the apostle does not seem to dichotomize exposition and evangelistic preaching *in the church* the way Mr. Murray might have us do so, nor did Martyn Lloyd-Jones. Writes Tony Sargent: "Lloyd-Jones wanted his congregation to be theologically literate: thus his concern to preach expositional sermons and his unqualified advice for younger preachers to attempt the same. Some of Lloyd-Jones's instructional sermons are very powerful."[27]

That said, Mr. Murray's concern that we not absolutize correct teaching is well taken. Besides looking for evangelistic opportunities in the exposition, we seek the fullness of the Spirit as

---

[27] Sargent, *The Sacred Anointing*, 256.

Mr. Murray counsels. Note how Paul, assuming Timothy has the Spirit (1:14), calls him nevertheless to "fan into flame the gift of God" (1:6). Consistent with this fanning is the depiction and thrust of New Testament terms for preaching.[28] Some of them cover non-preaching settings, but the terms include:

- *Aggelein*: To tell or to announce (normatively in the noun form of *aggelos*, messenger or angel, *passim*; or *aggelia*, message, doctrine, or precept [1 John 3:4]).

- *Anaggellein*: To bring back word, to report, to announce; to declare, set forth, or teach (Mark 5:14).

- *Kataggellein*: To announce, to proclaim, to laud, or to celebrate (Acts 13:38).

- *Apophtheggesthai*: To speak out or to declare (Acts 2:4, 14; 26:25).

- *Legein*: To speak, to address, to declare, to narrate, to put forth, to declare, to affirm (*passim*).

Most connected to preaching are:

- *Euaggelizomai*: To proclaim, to announce, or to address with good tidings.

- *Kērussō*: To publish, to proclaim (as a herald), to announce openly or publicly, to noise abroad, to preach.

Whereas the former is found only in the Gospels (in Matthew and especially in Luke), in Acts, profusely in Paul, on several occasions in (1) Peter, and a couple of times in Hebrews and Revelation, the latter is often found in Mark (1:4, 38, 45, 7:36, 13:10) and can be found in Luke's writings (Lk. 4:18, Acts 15:21), as well as in those of Paul (Rom 2:21; 1 Cor 9:27).

---

[28] In this paragraph I am indebted to Steven F. Davis's brief but excellent article, "The Doctrine of Preaching in the New Testament," available at http://www.biblicaltheology.com/Research/DavisS01.html, accessed May 27, 2014, and to *The Analytical Greek Lexicon Revised*, edited by Harold K. Moulton (Grand Rapids, MI: Regency Reference Library [Zondervan], 1978).

We could go on, suffice it to say that to one degree and another all these words hint at the Spirit's energy in driving preaching. Preaching is not less than teaching, but it is more than that, for it assumes conviction, passion, and excitement about the things of God and the message of his Word. We ought not to be embarrassed about expounding the Scriptures, but do acknowledge the need for it to be Spirit-driven. It is in the Spirit-filled proclamation and announcement that the teaching of the Word reaches the mind and touches the heart.

*c. The examples of Scripture:* Where do we see the New Testament's vocabulary for preaching better illustrated than in the ministry of Jesus and the apostle Paul? Whereas the former was full of the Spirit without measure (John 3:34), the latter was full of him to a remarkable degree.

While we do not justify from Scripture consecutive exposition from Christ's continuation of *lectio continua* (continuous reading) at the synagogue (Mark 1:21–28; Luke 4:16–21), such reading is nevertheless consistent with it. Writes William Hendrikson of Christ's teaching: "There was system in *his* preaching. As their [the scribes] Talmud proves, *they* often rambled on and on."[29] Nor do we claim that his application of the Hebrew Scriptures was a book-by-book justification and application of his Messiahship, yet it is interesting how systematic Jesus could be. Luke mentions two instances of it in relation to his resurrection. First, in 24:25–27 we read: "And beginning with Moses and all the Prophets, he interpreted to them in all the Scriptures the things concerning himself." And, again, in 24:44–47:

> Then he said to them, "These are my words that I spoke to you while I was still with you, that everything written about me in the Law of Moses and the Prophets and the Psalms must be fulfilled." Then he opened their minds to understand the Scriptures, and said to them, "Thus, it is written, that the Christ should suffer and on the third day rise from the dead, and that repentance and forgiveness of sins should be proclaimed in his name to all nations, beginning from Jerusalem.

---

[29] William Hendrikson, *The Gospel of Mark*, first published 1975; reprint ed. (Edinburgh: The Banner of Truth Trust, 1987, 63.

Then there is the example of Paul from his ministry to Jews and Gentiles. Recall, in the order of occurrence, how, when speaking to the intelligentsia in Athens (Acts 17:16–34), the apostle unpacked his sermon "text" most systemically, moving seamlessly through major *loci* of Biblical theology, touching on theology proper (the existence of God), creation, providence, salvation (the pursuit of God), and eschatology (the final judgment). Then, later in Rome, he calls the Jewish leaders together and "expounds" (*ezetitheto*, sets forth and proclaims) to them Jesus from their Scriptures, specifically from the Law and the Prophets, testifying to the kingdom of God, seeking to convince them of Jesus from morning till evening (Acts 28:23–24). Significantly, Paul failed to convince everyone, but kept on keeping on all the same: "He lived there [in Rome] two whole years at his own expense, and welcomed all who came to him, proclaiming the kingdom of God and teaching about the Lord Jesus Christ with all boldness and without hindrance" (28:30–31).

Paul evidently rolled into one historic ministry the faithfulness of the expositor, the passion of the evangelist, and the reasoning of the apologist—exactly the sort of ministry needed today! He mentored Timothy, his apostolic representative, to the same end, directing him to "follow the pattern [*upotupōsin*] of the sounds words" he had conveyed (2 Tim 1:13). The word Paul uses for "pattern" refers to a sketch, delineation, form, formula, model representation. While we do not know exactly what Paul's "sound words" were, we know they were structured and sufficiently clear to enable Timothy to pass them on to the next generation of teachers (2:2).

Together these important texts suggest various characteristics of Biblical preaching. Note in preaching that—
- The *scope* should be as extensive as the inspiration.
- *The structure* should consist of a delineation or sketch of the makeup of Scripture and of the contours of the great gospel revealed therein.
- The *exposition* should explain and apply the text.
- The *purpose* should range from the teaching of the gospel to the believer's training in righteousness.
- The *outreach* entails making Jesus known from both Testaments and from all the genres of Scripture.

- The *aim* is the salvation of children within the covenant community as well as of first-generation believers who enlarge it.
- The *empowerment* requires God's Spirit-filling and the preacher's habitual fanning into flame the gift of God's Spirit.
- The *freedom* permits and encourages the use of all Scripture for the sake of the exposition of the one unified gospel found therein.
- The *satisfaction* lies in having preached as many representative sections of the whole revealed counsel of God as is possible in any given ministry location.

Although the evidence, briefly considered, stops short of justifying the exclusive use of the systematic exposition of Biblical books—even supposing many of us are practicing this absolutely—it does reveal that consecutive exposition is consistent with the evidence and, well done, captures the spirit of such programmatic texts of Scripture. Paul's words surely make this point: "Until I come, devote yourself to the public reading of Scripture, to exhortation, to teaching. . . . Practice these things, immerse yourself in them, so that all may see your progress" (1 Tim 3:13, 15).

Several factors explain the differences between the preaching we find in Scripture and the expository preaching found in the church.

First, we must recall that much of the preaching mentioned in the sacred record was of an outdoor sort. Teaching was still prevalent in such contexts, but not necessarily exposition of a formal kind. Jesus' speech in his own name, demonstrating the fulfillment of the Law, and his introduction of parables to flummox the unbelieving (Matt 13:13), remind us that we are to draw our abiding homiletic principles chiefly from the didactic and not the descriptive portions of Scripture. To compare, for instance, the outdoor preaching of the Lord Jesus amid the plains and hills of Judea and Galilee with the indoor exposition of the present-day pulpit would be to compare apples and oranges. In each case the location and congregation determine the method. Greater commonality of method is derived and expected from the heeding of Paul's advice to his apostolic delegates in relation to the planting of first-century churches.

Secondly, we factor in the thought that the canon of Scripture is now complete—*practically* complete even if *hypothetically* open. Systematic or consecutive exposition feeds from this completeness. Would we expect to see, then, the consecutive exposition of Scripture prior to the writing or recognition of all the books of Scripture? Now that the canon is complete, the preacher can expound the Scriptures consecutively by means of either a thematic series rooted in the exposition of individual texts or of series proceeding through individual books in light of the canon *in toto*.[30]

### 3. *The reference to history.*

Iain Murray states that, "The best preaching is that which helps the hearers most, and in that connection the track record of the consecutive 'expository' method is not impressive. It has never proved popular in the long term, and the reason for that, I think, is clear: A sermon needs a text as the basis for a memorable message." Now since our esteemed friend is coy about whom he is correcting, and supplies no criteria or evidence for his criticism of consecutive exposition, it is difficult to attest his viewpoint. We can offer, however, a general response, feeling the need to do so since by his opacity Mr. Murray brings the work of all consecutive expositors under scrutiny. Specifically, I question—

*a. His basis of assessment:* What helps the hearers most and is popular are criteria simplistically stated. We may ask, for instance, which hearers are we are talking about?

If these are unconverted hearers—for Mr. Murray would rightly have us reach them—since when has any mode of preaching been inevitably deemed helpful or popular? Try telling Noah that what helps the hearer most will please him best! Or Jesus, since his death reveals he had but 120 disciples left in Jerusalem and 500 in Galilee. And what of today's preacher who does not practice

---

[30] Stott points to this variety in consecutive exposition in *The Preacher's Portrait*, 23.

consecutive exposition but has a ministry deemed no more helpful or popular than one who does? Should he, on the basis of the criteria helpfulness and of popularity, leave off all exposition, and go anecdotal instead? While we pray that faithfulness to the Word will lead to fruitfulness, it is difficult to see how this reasoning escapes the charge of pragmatism (if it works it must be right). Such pragmatism, if that is what it is, is antithetical to the Reformed faith for it pits the experiential in "experiential Calvinism" against the Calvinism. It also misappropriates church history, for Mr. Murray is judging the popularity of preaching outside of revival by what went on inside it, and thus does nothing for the expositor seeking to be both faithful and fruitful in the present regardless of the type of exposition he utilizes.

Mr. Murray has more of a case for weighing what is helpful and popular if, alternatively, he is thinking of converted hearers. They, like the preacher, have the Spirit of Christ within, and can discern what they need, and what they need can in fact be popular. But it still does not always follow that way. What about fledgling believers who are only just beginning to learn what they need from the Word? Or, back-slid believers who know what they need, but don't want it? Or, naïve believers fed by spiritual fast-food all week (anecdotal preaching, edited radio segments, or truncated YouTube clips), and want the same on Sunday? I am not saying that systematic expositors have a monopoly on what their hearers need, nor that personal unpopularity should always be explained away as the hearer's problem. But Mr. Murray pays no attention to the fact that the pastor, called of God, listening out for God all week, bold enough to go against the fads of the moment, may in fact have the mind of the Spirit in regard to what his people need, despite the fact that it is not immediately popular. This is especially so in church revitalizations, where the power of the Word, despite the want of popularity of the preacher, is gradually sorting out the church.

All in all, then, it seems there's need of more balance between the respective responsibilities of the preacher and the congregant than Mr. Murray offers. For that, consult T. H. L. Parker's treatment of *Calvin's Preaching*. He notes how the Reformer saw proclamation as a joint enterprise between the pastor and his people: The more the people understood the nature of preaching, the more they would attend to it.[31] This has been the experience of many a consecutive expositor since Calvin's day. As congregants adapt to the method of systematic exposition, they come to miss a given series when a break is taken from it. They yearn for the next installment, because their appetite for Scripture has been enlarged.[32]

*b. His boldness of assessment:* Judge for yourself whether the track record of systematic exposition is unimpressive. John Stott, a leading expositor of the twentieth century, points us to Chrysostom, the great systematic expositor of the first four centuries; to Luther, Zwingli, Bullinger, and Calvin most systematically of all. He refers thereafter to Matthew Henry, whose expositions over a twenty-five-year period led to his renowned Commentary on the whole Bible;[33] to the expositions of Charles Simeon and, later, of the likes of Joseph Parker and Alexander Maclaren.[34] Similarly, Hughes Oliphant Old, a leading authority on the history of preaching in the Christian church, writes:

> As the history of preaching is unfolded, it becomes clear how important the orderly, systematic preaching through the

---

[31] For a flavor of Calvin's view and Parker's treatment, see Joe Morecraft III's review titled, "The Pulpit as the Throne of God," in *The Counsel of Chalcedon* (January/February, 1994), 29–30. It is available at http://chalcedon.org/docs/counselpdf/1994_1%20Book%20Review,%20Calvins%20Preaching%20by%20T.H.L.%20Parker.pdf, accessed May 28, 2014.

[32] In noting how in consecutive exposition the "mind of God is discovered more accurately in the precise statements, proportions, and connexions of truth," Bridges makes the interesting observation that "the course of family worship would materially assist the moulding of the mind into this scheme" (*The Christian Ministry*, 285). It is perhaps the decline of family worship which helps explain the difficulty in acclimating congregants to consecutive exposition. Conversely, the method is very well suited to influence the recovery of family worship.

[33] In fairness, Stott's reference to Henry must be offset against the opinion of J. B. Williams in his *Memoirs of the Life, Character, and Writings of the Rev. Matthew Henry* in J. B. Williams, *The Lives of Philip and Matthew Henry*, (two volumes in one), first published 1828 (Edinburgh and Carlisle, PA, 1974), 119: "With regard to variety [of preaching], Mr. Henry avoided the practice of many 'ancient worthies,' who, having chosen a subject for the pulpit, pursued it, week after week, from the *same* text. He preferred employing different texts for the discussion of even the same general truth; and improvement well adapted to relieve both the preacher and the hearers from the wearisome insipidity inseparable from continued iteration."

[34] Stott, *I Believe in Preaching*, 317–19; *The Preacher's Portrait*, 22–25.

scriptures has been a favorite system of preaching over the centuries. One is surprised to discover how many of history's great preachers made a regular practice of preaching through one book of the Bible after another. Origen, the first Christian preacher from whom we have any sizable collection of sermons, preached most of his sermons on the *lectio continua*. We find the same with John Chrysostom who is usually referred to as the greatest Christian preacher. We find the same true of Augustine as well. At the time of the Protestant Reformation Zwingli, Calvin, Bucer and John Knox followed this system regularly, and they passed it on to the Puritans. Today we see a real revival of *lectio continua* preaching.[35]

Mr. Murray either has to play down the influence of Martyn Lloyd-Jones as a *consecutive* expositor, or imply that his brilliance was such that none can emulate him (see below). But to do that he has to forget, to mention the few, James Montgomery Boice whose consecutive exposition could be heard across America for thirty years; the long-standing excellence of the warmhearted Scotsman Eric Alexander; John MacArthur, about whom he has written a biography; and Alistair Begg, described as the Scottish evangelist— yes, evangelist!—of America.[36] Are they part of the unimpressive track record?

And what of the countless lesser-known ministers who, using the method of consecutive exposition, heed Paul's charge to Timothy to "preach the Word," being "ready in season and out of season" (2 Tim 4:2)? Is their track record to be deemed unimpressive because they don't have the results of revival and must, like Timothy, "reprove, rebuke, and exhort with complete patience and teaching"? Perhaps expositors are at their most impressive when, obedient to Paul's call to persist (1 Tim 3:16), they keep to their task in a day when "people will not endure sound teaching, but having itching ears they will accumulate for themselves teachers to suit their own

---

[35] Hughes Oliphant Old, endorsement of *The Lectio Continua Expository Commentary Series*, published at http://lectiocontinua.com/, accessed May 24, 2014.

[36] Specifically, MacArthur writes: "Through more than three decades of ministry at Grace Community Church, I have had the privilege of presenting expositional sermons almost every Sunday. I have preached systematically through one book of the Bible on Sunday mornings and a different book on Sunday evenings" (*The Battle for the Beginning: The Bible on Creation and the Fall of Adam* [W Publishing Group, 2001]), 9).

passions," and as a result "endure suffering" to fulfill their ministry (2 Tim 4:3 and 5).

*c. His reasoning of assessment:* A sermon needs a text, says Mr. Murray, as the basis of a memorable message. There's some truth to this, but, again, it is difficult to see why this must negate systematic exposition. Is it not possible, quite typical even, to build a sermon from the context of the previous week to the central or climactic text of the current verses, succeeding in the process of making all the passage memorable without stealing the thunder of the text for which the passage is known? After all, the light shed by the context of a consecutive exposition can bring its own fascination. Conversely, it is not unknown for an individual text to suffer de-contextualization in order for it to sustain its memorability in the popular mind.

I recall from my twenties hearing a minister used in Banner of Truth circles preaching Revelation 3:20 disconnectedly: "Behold, I stand at the door and knock. If anyone hears my voice and opens the door, I will come to him and eat with him, and he with me." He began his sermon with the words, almost verbatim: "I know the text is addressed to Christians, but I am going to use it to speak to the non-Christian." Undoubtedly, Mr. Murray does not want to uphold this sort of approach, nor should The Banner of Truth Trust be tarred by such a puzzling abuse of the text by an otherwise good man. But consecutive exposition, rightly done, does not necessitate the sacrifice of a text to the degree Mr. Murray fears, nor does the choice of an individual text ensure that the sermon will be memorable, let alone for the right reasons. Certainly, there is something special about the Spirit's enabling to preach a text memorably, but there are liabilities to avoid whether we preach a text in sequence or not. If Mr. Murray bases his argument against consecutive exposition on really the distortion of the method, as he goes on to do, I see no reason why it cannot be defended on the basis, in part, of the way individual texts are sometimes preached.

Regardless which expository method we use, it's worth asking whether Mr. Murray is according memorability too much weight. When critics of the awakenings of Jonathan Edwards's day alleged that much of what was heard was not recalled, Edwards rejoined: "The main benefit that is obtained by preaching is by impression made upon the mind in the time of it, and not by the effect that arises afterwards by a remembrance of what was delivered."[37] Marsden adds, "Preaching, in other words, must first touch the affections." It must also be nourishing—another evidence of good preaching not necessarily implying memorability. A letter appearing in the *British Weekly* ran as follows and illustrates the point: "It seems ministers feel their sermons are very important and spend a great deal of time preparing them. I have attended church regularly for 30 years and I have probably heard 3,000 of them. To my dismay, I discovered I can't remember a single sermon. I wonder if a minister's time might be more profitable spent on something else?" According to John Ross's recounting of this anecdote, the letter unleashed a storm of responses, which finally ended with this one: "I have been married for 30 years. During that time I have eaten 32,850 meals, mostly my wife's cooking. But I cannot remember the menu of a single meal. And yet I have the distinct impression that without them, I would have starved to death long ago."[38] The point is striking. Not every sermon can be memorable whichever method we use, but all must be nourishing.

Consecutive or systematic exposition can be memorable and ought to touch the affections—not forgetting that it is intermingled with the preaching of individual texts—but series preaching wins hands down when it comes to balanced and hearty nourishment.

4. *The overlooking of pastoral factors.*

Various problems are associated with assessing systematic exposition chiefly in terms of souls converted and numbers gathered. In a day of so-called small things, this uni or chiefly unidimensional criterion overlooks the manifold purpose of God in any given pastoral situation.

A minister may come, for instance, to *a congregation which is very religious but carnal.* Is he to assume that if the congregation finds his expositions dull that the problem lies with him? What if the

---

[37] Quoted by George M. Marsden in *Jonathan Edwards: A Life* (New Haven and London: Yale University Press, 2003), 282.

[38] Dr. Ross posted this to his Facebook page on May 17, 2014, accessed last on May 21, 2014.

congregation has those itching ears Paul mentions, wanting only what's palatable or personally applicable, and has lost sight of the fact that worship is first and foremost about God? The minister, sticking as closely as possible to revealed truth, may find initially that he empties rather than fills the church. Sometimes God calls his people to tear down before they can build up, as the Reformers did. It won't be pleasant nor win him celebrity status in the eyes of the wider church, but the consecutive exposition will have done its work. This is why Calvin connects courage and the homiletic method, "—not courage to believe but courage to proclaim the truth, however, unpalatable, and to rebuke where rebukes are necessary. It is inevitable that he will arouse opposition: 'They that intend to serve God faithfully and to proclaim His Word will never lack enemies to make war against them. . . . Insomuch that the man who serves God in bearing His Word faithfully will never have peace nor go without stings and unmolested, nor be without many enemies.'"[39] Stott makes the same connection.[40] Let these "two or three witnesses" establish the fact, then, that it takes bravery to keep expounding under such circumstances, and also faith to believe the work will be divinely vindicated, albeit on God's terms and in his timing.

Alternatively, a minister may come to *a pious and spiritually minded congregation*, but one more familiar with devotional sermonettes on the one hand or catechetical preaching on the other. It will take some years to acclimate the congregation to systemic preaching, however wisely the minister introduces it. I recall, for example, an elder whose judgment on issues of preaching I cherish, saying to me shortly into my time at the church, "When you follow the method of consecutive exposition you really have to preach the difficult texts, don't you?" We were going through the Epistle of James at the time and tackling the searching indictment he gives of the use of the tongue (3:1–12). Around the same time I visited a couple who were homebound. The husband, a dear brother, is an avid listener to the radio broadcast and a faithful prayer warrior. He blurted out: "Couldn't you say something more positive about the tongue?" "When James does!" I replied. On the way out of the door, his wife

---

[39] From Sermon 194 (Deut 33:ll [*CO* 29.154]), cited in Morecraft, "The Pulpit as the Throne of God," 28.
[40] Stott, *I Believe in Preaching*, 315–16.

whispered to me: "The sermon was too close to home." Seven years on, I rejoice in every member of our church who, in the continental Reformed environment of Western Michigan, has chosen to allow God's Word to come through their minds to their hearts. It has not been comfortable (or universally popular!), and some have reacted verbally or with their feet; but there are those testifying that the experience has been for their health, while others have joined us for the expositions, some in the sanctuary and others via the radio broadcasts.

In either scenario, or any other for that matter, the preacher will learn from the feedback. The way he is misunderstood in the church can breed clarity, and the way he is slandered without breeds character. His perseverance will be for the benefit of his hearers, as will his patient learning of his craft. Along the way he will pick up insight about the congregation he serves, and the trust of an eldership which believes faithfulness can, with God's blessing, lead to fruitfulness in the end. On this understanding, I ponder how many of the instances Mr. Murray deems disastrous consequences of consecutive exposition were occasioned by insufficient support for the expositor and understanding of expository preaching. When a soccer manager, for example, is fired amid his revitalization of a club because recent results have gone against the team, we are robbed of the opportunity to see what might have been. Typically we find that great managers were given time. Ask Sir Alex Ferguson of Manchester United fame. He came, apparently, within one game of being fired early in his time at Old Trafford. How much more do ministers of the Word need time, for their schedule is the Lord's and not their own!

5. *The neglect of evangelistic complexities.*

Since we have seen from Paul's ministry in Rome that evangelism can be done amid exposition, the question we now consider is how we may best approach it. Fundamentally, there are two types of unbeliever to bear in mind: the churched and the unchurched.

The churched take priority. From Old Testament times the emphasis in public worship was on the assembly. The Hebrew *Qahal* is the Old Testament equivalent of the New Testament use of "church"—the *ekklesia* or the called-out ones. The principles of the old covenant era carry over into the new, unless abrogated. Contrary to the notion that the baptized are already regenerate and that there is, in effect, no difference between being a child of the covenant and being a child of God, the liturgy for infant baptism at the church I serve states that covenant children, once baptized, are "engaged to confess the faith of Christ crucified." In other words, they possess the privileges of the covenant community, but also the responsibilities of believing the gospel of Jesus and repenting from sin. Until they do so, they remain like unbelieving Jews who were descended from Israel but did not belong to Israel (Rom 9:6). They are in the visible church, but not of her.

For the sake of baptized members alone, I would gladly dedicate a weekly evangelistic sermon as did Lloyd-Jones, but there are certain challenges with that practice.

In continental Reformed churches the implied or stated teaching of presumptive regeneration has gone very deep. In consequence of this there is a lingering assumption among some that every member of the visible church is born again. Although beautiful in itself, the opening Question and Answer of the Heidelberg Catechism—"What is your only comfort, in life and in death?"—does nothing to dispel the presumption and neither does the preacher's sermon on Lord's Day 1 unless handled discerningly.[41] In some such churches the call to believe and to repent jars. Certain congregants interpret the call as the minister's belief that few congregants are Christian, while others feel it erodes the members'

---

[41] The Heidelberg Catechism Q. 1 asks, "What is your only comfort, in life and in death?" What the answer possesses in terms of personal warmth, it lacks in terms of God-centeredness: "That *I* belong . . . to *my* faithful Savior, Jesus Christ, who . . . has fully paid for all *my* sins, and has completely freed *me* from the dominion of the devil; that he protects *me* so well, that without *my* Father . . . not a hair can fall from *my* head . . . *my* salvation . . . assures *me* of eternal life, and makes *me* wholeheartedly willing and ready from now on to live for him." Ten times it refers to us, but only eight times to the Trinity. By contrast Westminster Shorter Catechism asks, "What is the chief end of man?" And the answer is: "The chief end of man is to glorify God and to enjoy him forever." Or, as John Piper revises the answer: "The chief end of man is to glorify God *by* enjoying him forever." The question elicits an answer which is chiefly about God, and refers to him twice and to us once.

assurance, or spoils the unity of the church family. Such resistance to evangelistic preaching is born of the mistaken idea that adherence to the church equates to allegiance to Christ. While the rush to preach a weekly evangelistic sermon makes, in principle, great sense in such a context, consecutive exposition suffused with the gospel call likely does a better job explaining why the call to repent and to believe is necessary. The method of preaching also wards off the likelihood of a total exodus to churches where the false comfort of presumptive regeneration is alive and well.

Alternatively, in churches not of the continental Reformed persuasion, there is the challenge of finding the fine line of promoting the gospel without encouraging gospel hardening. When week after week and year after year attendees at church refuse the gospel call, the preacher must determine the point at which a weekly evangelistic sermon begins to cast the pearls of the gospel before the metaphorical "swine" (Matt 7:6).

Why not preach the great gospel texts all the same, one a week, for the sake of the unchurched who visit worship? After all, our public assemblies across the Reformed world are overwhelmingly open assemblies to which the unchurched are invited, even if public worship was ordained with the person "in the pew" in mind rather than the "person on the street." In support of such questions, Iain Murray would have us contemplate the practice of his two prominent examples: Spurgeon and Lloyd-Jones.

For all that we love and admire these brothers in Christ, it is worth asking whether Mr. Murray has forgotten to contextualize their ministries. They were of the modern era, albeit the closure of it in Lloyd-Jones's case. Folk were still generally accepting of the context of truth, even if they sought to access it by reason rather than through faith. The church doors were open with greater hope that folk from outside would enter and stay. Thus, it made sense for Lloyd-Jones to preach one end of the Lord's Day an evangelistic sermon, for he could guarantee a hearing. The fact of the matter is that we will never know how Spurgeon or Lloyd-Jones would have fared in the challenges of ongoing crumbling church attendance in Europe.

That said, the unchurched continue to walk into churches today. They do, for God is sovereign, the Lord's people still bring friends along, and LED signs and other advertising seem to have some effect. But it is very clear in this postmodern era, given the widening gap between the cultures of church and society, that Sunday worship may not be the first point of contact an unbeliever has or wants with us. As many churches have experienced, they may be more likely to join in a church social event, a small Bible study, a *Christianity Explored* course, *Griefshare* or *Divorce Care* ministry. In the postmodern era the seeker looks initially for the believer's authenticity and relational sincerity, not least through hospitality. Without the church family building trust, the leadership in particular (1 Tim 3:2), the seeker is not likely to take seriously what the unknown figure fronting worship has to say. He may speak with authority, but does not have the seeker's trust automatically. If we fail to understand this, and plug away on the basis of the older model, as numerous conservative Reformed churches do, simply waiting for a Spurgeonic or Lloyd-Jonesian era to return, we preachers will find ourselves with evangelistic sermon in hand, only to find congregants either not faithful in bringing unconverted along, or feeling guilty that they have tried but without success. Scanning the congregation for unchurched visitors, the minister, for his part, feels saddened and frustrated that his sermon on the great gospel text, even if blessed, reaches but the few, and runs the risk meanwhile of irritating communicant members, effecting gospel hardening in baptized members, or both.

This is not a situation I justify, but it is reality in conservative Reformed churches which have either not understood the cultural changes or ignored them. While the preaching of a gospel sermon may over time encourage more outreach-mindedness in a congregation, and fulfill God's purposes in hardening the non-elect (Acts 28:25–27), why should a minister not continue his systematic expositions at both services (where applicable) in the event of a settled inability to connect the lost to Lord's Day worship, especially when the good news of Jesus runs through each message of the consecutive exposition and is brought home by means of the proclamation? Can we not, then, offset Mr. Murray's concern by informing the church family that:

- They ought to bring their contacts to church any way they can. If they will come to public worship, all well and good, but they may come through the series of stepping stones the church has in place.
- The consecutive exposition is continuing morning and evening, and which of the series in progress is likely to help visitors the most. While God is able to save his elect at either service, one service may be more *apropos* to the needs of the unchurched visitor than the other.
- Breaks from the exposition will be taken for Christmas and Easter, for example, and special invitations will be sent out for these high points of the outreach. The big gospel texts will be preached.

In these ways we may both feed the believer and reach the unregenerate from both churched and unchurched contexts, without counter-productivity to the DNA of the church or to those we seek to reach.

David Wells reminds us, however, that in order to be effective in the lives of those who come under our ministries, we need to pay attention to the importance of both the text and context.[42] Preaching lives between the two worlds of the Biblical text and of our minds and daily life. Exposition cannot be, then, but a protest against other homiletic methods, nor an aping of sermons from a bygone era replete with application as if we still live in the Reformation and Puritan eras—which is a temptation for some most romantically or idealistically hooked on Reformed reprints. We cannot afford there to be too much truth in the witticism once aired about the Westminster Conference in London, namely, that it seeks "to prepare the twentieth-century Christian minister for whatever the seventeenth century could throw at him."[43] I do not urge the devaluing of Reformed reprints, only their application to a context in the West more akin to the first and second centuries than the

---

[42] David F. Wells, *The Courage to Be Protestant: Truth-lovers, Marketeers, and Emergents in the Postmodern World* (Grand Rapids, MI, and Cambridge, UK: William B. Eerdmans, 2008), 229–33.

[43] Davies, *Genius, Grief and Grace*, 360.

fifteenth and sixteenth. To achieve this, our exegesis must detect the intersection at which an effective bridge can be constructed to connect the ancient text to the world of today.

### 6. *The matter of priorities.*

We ponder here whether Mr. Murray's swinging of his weight against the current prevalence of consecutive exposition in certain circles is advisable at a time when Biblical illiteracy is greater overall, it seems, than in any period since the eighteenth century, if not since prior to the Reformation. Did Mr. Murray not think of the worlds of *liberal, evangelical,* and *Reformed Protestantism* when offering his caution?

*a. Liberal Protestantism.* Need we say anything more of pulpit ministry in a context wherein the "gospel" has been so adequately and famously summarized by H. Richard Niebuhr (1894–1962) as "a God without wrath [who] brought men without sin into a kingdom without judgment through the ministrations of a Christ without a Cross"? Since, however, Mr. Murray's voice would neither reach, interest, nor convince those of such a persuasion, we cannot in all fairness critique him for not aiming his caution at liberal preaching. All the same, we do ponder whether a regular diet of consecutive exposition is the main homiletic problem today.

*b. Evangelical Protestantism.* Regularly fed these days on little more than self-help anecdotal motivational speaking, with sound bites of Scripture and theology thrown in, it seems to me that Mr. Murray could have done a greater service to the church in his comments. After all, which weighs heavier, the need for less consecutive exposition or the need for the spread of it? Listen to Calvin's sermon on Mic 3:7:

> For what ought sermons and doctrines to be, except expositions of what Scripture contains? Truly, if we add the slightest nuance, it only results in corruption. Our Lord has left us a perfect doctrine in the Law, the Prophets, and the Gospels. Thus, what ought we to be preaching today? We ought not to be adding anything new to the text, but ought to be providing a clearer exposition that would confirm our understandings of God's teachings. That, I repeat, is the purpose of any sermon or lecture we hear, that we might each

be better instructed with respect to God's will. That way, whenever we hear anything, we have a basis for inquiring whether God has spoken or not. By the same token, all who are charged with preaching God's Word know that it is wrong of them to add anything of their own, or anything they might invent. They must be certain that what they preach is not of their own conjecture but derives from God, who guides them on the basis of his certain and infallible Word.[44]

To understand how far standards of preaching have fallen from the bar set by Calvin, consider David Wells' citation of James Singleton's statistics pertaining to two hundred ostensibly evangelical sermons appearing in the *Pulpit Digest* (January–February 1981 to March–April 1991) and *Preaching* (July–August 1985 to January–February 1991). In 24.5% the content and organization were determined by the Biblical passage under consideration. In 22.5% the content was explicitly Biblical, but the preacher took the liberty of imposing his or her organization upon it. In 39% neither the content nor organization arose from a Biblical passage, although the content was recognizably Biblical. In 14% neither the content nor organization arose from a Biblical passage nor were discernibly Christian. In total, fewer than half were explicitly Biblical, and only one in seven was even discernibly Christian.[45] Hence the question whether a regular diet of consecutive exposition is really what requires caution today.

*c. Reformed Protestantism* (i.e. the continental Reformed practice of catechetical preaching). While Mr. Murray quotes R. B. Kuiper on what is in effect the abuse of exposition (the distortion of the running commentary), he omits to do so in regard to the drawbacks of catechetical preaching: the confusion of our source of authority in preaching on the one hand, and of doctrinal (expository) and doctrinaire (catechetical) preaching on the other. Writes Kuiper, catechetical preaching, "however excellently intended, is in at least some danger of running afoul of the *Scriptura sola* principle." He continues:

---

[44] I am indebted to local theology student Confex Makhalira for this quotation. Go to: https://conmakhalira.wordpress.com/2014/06/10/lessons-from-john-calvins-method-of-preaching/, accessed on June 10, 2014.

[45] David F. Wells, *God in the Wasteland: The Reality of Truth in a World of Fading Dreams* (Leicester, England: Inter-Varsity and Grand Rapids, MI: William B. Eerdmans, 1994), 149fn.

> . . . doctrinal preaching, like all preaching, must be based upon
> the Word of God, and that is a way of saying that it may not
> be based upon the creeds . . . the church's interpretation of
> Scripture is fallible, and so its confessions of faith and
> catechisms can do no more than serve as helpful guides in
> preaching. Never may they be regarded as the source of
> doctrine or the touchstone of truth. Those distinctions belong
> to the Bible alone. And he who makes use of the creeds in
> preaching is in sacred duty bound to keep that fact
> unmistakably clear.[46]

While subordinate standards are useful at specific points in the
process of exposition for articulating Biblical truth, this use precludes
the obscuring of the Scripture's sole authority for faith and conduct.

How do we explain Mr. Murray's decision to caution against
the prevalence of consecutive exposition? I am not sure. The most
generous interpretation, and possibly the right one, is that Mr.
Murray shares a passion for Biblical exposition, and is just concerned
that it not be brought into disrepute by too much consecutive
exposition. On this understanding, we jointly favor exposition and
wish to spare it from abuses. But whereas Mr. Murray thinks a
combination of less consecutive exposition and more exposition of
individual texts is the beginning of a corrective, it seems to me that to
throw out the numerous weighty reasons for expounding the
Scriptures systematically for the preaching of disconnected texts,
when a regular diet of consecutive exposition already includes the
preaching of disconnected texts, is a counterproductive overkill and
is potentially harmful to the church.

A less favorable interpretation pertains to the aftermath of
the 1970 split in the Puritan Conference.[47] While the reasons for the

---

[46] Cited by G. I. Williamson, "Some Thoughts on Preaching," *Ordained Servant*, 3:2
(April, 1994) and available on-line at http://opc.org/OS/html/V3/2c.html,
accessed May 26, 2014. Williamson's quotation of R. B. Kuiper is taken from *The
Infallible Word: A Symposium by the Members of the Faculty of Westminster Theological
Seminary* (Philipsburg, NJ: Presbyterian and Reformed Publishing Company, 1980),
227–229.

[47] A brief synopsis of the origin of the Puritan Conference, which dates back to
1951 and was rebranded as the Westminster Conference in 1971, is found at
http://www.westminsterconference.org.uk/history/, accessed May 29, 2014. A

breakup involving Dr. Lloyd-Jones and Dr. Packer are not our interest here, I note Gaius Davies's courageous claim regarding its aftereffects.[48] Dr. Lloyd-Jones shrunk, he says, from being a great leader to the head of a party. Now, assuming this is true, Mr. Murray, by dint of his personal contact with Dr. Lloyd-Jones and his status as official biographer, is about as senior as they come in the "party" today. While it is made up of confessional Presbyterians, Baptists, and Congregationalists, The Banner of Truth Trust—sometimes referred to informally as the mother of all Reformed publishers—is most pursuant of the doctrines of grace and a love of the experiential Calvinism of the Puritans. However, there are many evangelical Anglicans who have arisen in the United Kingdom and Australia who are heavily into consecutive exposition and are very adept at opening up Scripture, but do not always resonate the experiential emphasis of the Banner of Truth publications with their combination of experiential Calvinism on the one hand and a heavy dose of Celtic (Scottish, Irish, and Welsh) influence on the other.

It is possible, then, that Mr. Murray's caution speaks to this variation of Reformed evangelical outlook. His more recent piece on the 2014 T4G Conference suggests he has in mind the circles of the Proclamation Trust, for in it he takes to task in his gentrified way David Jackman, past president of Proclamation Trust, for what he perceives to be a veiled critique of Dr. Lloyd-Jones.[49] A less defensive reading of David Jackman suggests that all he is saying is that Biblical exposition and worship style need to be in the musical and rhetorical style and cadence of today's world rather than that of the 1960s. He's not calling, then, for the compromising of principles but for the

---

fuller summary is found in the Publisher's Introduction to D. M. Lloyd-Jones, *The Puritans: Their Origins and Successors (Addresses Delivered at the Puritan and Westminster Conferences, 1959–1978)*, (Edinburgh and Carlisle, PA: The Banner of Truth Trust, 1987), vii–xiii.

[48] Gaius Davies, *Genius, Grief and Grace,* 359ff.

[49] Cf. Iain H. Murray, "Thoughts on 'The Together for the Gospel' Conference 2014," (http://banneroftruth.org/us/resources/articles/2014/thoughts-together-gospel-conference-2014/, accessed June 10, 2014), and David Jackman's column "Notes to Growing Christians," *Evangelicals Now* (February 2014), 21 (https://evangelicalsnow.wordpress.com/category/notes-to-growing-christians/, accessed June 10, 2014). Go to http://www.proctrust.org.uk/ for more on the ministry of the Proclamation Trust.

adjustment of the preferences pertaining to their packaging:

> The challenge for us . . . is how to communicate biblical truth in the changed cultures of the 21st century, without diminution of the biblical context, or accommodation of the message to the prejudices of the listeners. That's a challenge faced not only by every preacher, but every Sunday school teacher, youth worker, study group leader; indeed every individual believer who is trying to share their faith.

Mr. Murray, however, may well have been stung by other words of David Jackman which appear to be as relevant to him as to Dr. Lloyd-Jones:

> The temptation of those of us who remember a different style and presentation of even evangelical truth, is to fantasise nostalgically that the "pulpit greats" of the past might be emulated today. But, of course, if they were of today's generation their approach would be entirely different. Like all good preachers, they were of their time, speaking both from and into their own culture, which was so much more Christian than ours today.

Instead of grappling with the current challenges to preaching, distinguishing Biblical principle and personal preference, Mr. Murray opts to sustain what some of us who remain enamored by the Banner of Truth might these days see as a needless dichotomy between those in the party and those outside of it. We laud Mr. Murray's balanced emphasis on Word and Spirit in worship and in preaching specifically, and own his emphasis on preaching in faith and in the power of the Spirit, but ponder his *modus operandi* in defending his corner. In particular, he seems to offer some slack to the T4G conference which he withholds from David Jackman.[50] Additionally,

---

[50] I particularly query Mr. Murray's statement about the T4G Conference that, "no ground was given to the cry that 'we are in the visual age, not in the age of the spoken word,'" when the conference was fronted by a huge screen. I make no criticism of the screen, and with such numbers can only imagine how one was needed to aid the reception of the preaching. But I smile at Mr. Murray's comment, given that any use of a screen can be understood in Grand Rapids as the defining mark of liberalism! I also wonder to what degree Mr. Murray's assessments of the conference would match those of the individual churches represented. My point is not to raise questions in this regard. I simply wonder whether Mr. Murray is applying the same yardstick to the T4G Conference (inclusive of speakers wearing

he pays little attention to the differences between the American and British contexts, and the fact that, with few exceptions, in the Middle States of America the march to secularization lags significantly behind the pace and spread of it in the United Kingdom.

So what am I saying? Basically, that there is need for a coming together within British Reformed evangelicalism, not least over the matter of preaching. Those inside and outside "the party" can find more ground to share by regarding preaching as a three- rather than a two-legged stool. If impressions are at all accurate, preaching in Banner of Truth circles is characterized by the legs of textual faithfulness and Spirit enabling, while the Proclamation Trust and evangelical Anglicanism stress textual faithfulness and cultural relevance. Yet, is it so impossible for our preaching to stand on all three legs—textual faithfulness, cultural relevance, and the Spirit's filling—no matter the circles in which we move? Speaking personally, I stand with the evangelical Anglicans in regard to their emphasis on consecutive exposition, but wish to see encouraged the Murrayite stress on the ministry and influence of the Holy Spirit in preaching. Conversely, I laud Rev. Murray and Dr. Lloyd-Jones for upholding the spirituality of preaching, while nevertheless finding John Stott's perception of the Spirit's ministry and work to be more hermeneutically reliable and textually accurate. On this understanding, I argue that a return to Scripture and not simply to our extra-Biblical heroes is what is needed if we are to forge a more united way forward.

---

jeans) as he is to David Jackman's vision of expository preaching today.

# 4 CONCLUSION

> For the health of the Church (which lives and flourishes by the Word of God) and for the help of the preacher (who needs this discipline), it is urgent to return to systematic exposition.
>
> John R. W. Stott, *I Believe in Preaching*

Such an analysis of Mr. Murray's brief caution may seem like overkill. Possibly it is, but probably not. Firstly, the length of this response is governed by the richness of the array of issues Mr. Murray raises or implies. Secondly, it is easier for Mr. Murray to make the caution than for those responding to answer it. If Tom says that Dick killed Harry, you can imagine how disproportionate the response will be to the actual charge. This is especially so when all the factors involved in the charge are taken into account. Likewise, we have gone into detail considering the warranted aspects of Mr. Murray's concerns before analyzing what has been infelicitous in his point of view and questionable in its airing. We have found in summary that Mr. Murray's caution is worth pondering sincerely, but I am not convinced it bears sufficient weight to encourage responsible expositors to jettison systematic exposition.

Consider three matters:

1. *The big picture.*

It seems to me that Mr. Murray argues—

Firstly, the *wrong line.* Had he simply warned against the abuse of expository preaching, that would be fair enough; for the expositor is the last person who wishes the method brought into disrepute. But to seek to influence a withdrawal from what John Stott has called "the value of systematic exposition,"[51] goes too far.

Secondly, in the *wrong way.* A strong case does not need the utilizing of special pleading (stacking the deck in favor of his argument), unnecessary dichotomies, at least one extraordinarily dubious claim, a perspective rooted in the modern rather than the postmodern context, and the omission of the liabilities of nonconsecutive exposition.

Thirdly, at the *wrong time.* If the biggest problem with preaching today were consecutive exposition poorly done or done in the wrong contexts, then Mr. Murray's timing would be fine. But to try and scale back the popularity of consecutive exposition in a day of such Biblical illiteracy and the widespread predominance of anecdotal preaching on the one hand, and of the dangers of the inordinate elevation of confessional standards *vis-à-vis* Scripture in the catechetical method seems counterproductive.

Fourthly, to the *wrong readership.* His focus bespeaks, proverbially, a straining at the gnat and a swallowing of the camel. There is far more good than harm being done by consecutive exposition, and far more harm than good being done in wider evangelicalism by a regular diet of anecdotal preaching. Ministering at the epicenter of Dutch Reformed

---

[51] Stott, *I Believe in Preaching*, 315.

life in North America, I am also concerned about the drawbacks of the catechetical method. By structuring the preaching schedule, the Heidelberg Catechism tends to challenge, even if unwittingly, the supreme authoritative role of Scripture, and truncates in the process the congregant's exposure to it. The catechetical method loses the proportionate emphases of Scripture (influencing a me-ism with its lopsided emphasis on comfort), as also Scripture's multi-genre character. Understandably, the Heidelberg Catechism bespeaks the historic Eurocentrism of the tradition. This does not detract from the Catechism's beauty and faithfulness, but it does admit without cover-up that the Catechism, as a human document, can never compete with the theopneustic origin and authoritative qualities of Scripture.

More familiar with Banner of Truth circles than those of evangelical Anglicanism or the Proclamation Trust, I must, given these hang-ups, go with John Stott on this one: "For the health of the Church (which lives and flourishes by the Word of God) and for the help of the preacher (who needs this discipline), it is urgent to return to systematic exposition."[52] The completed canon allows for it, the profitability of all Scripture encourages it, and the history of Reformation preaching supports it. Consecutive exposition is the true heir of Reformation preaching,

2. *The big task.*

Whether we are returning to systematic exposition or setting out to learn the method, Mr. Murray's caution offers us some take-away points. I speak chiefly to myself in saying:

*Let Us*:

- Always love God more than the text of Scripture. One is the almighty Creator, the other a creation, albeit holy and

---

[52] Stott, *I Believe in Preaching*, 319.

infallible.

- Always make room for gospel application, for the Scripture speaks supremely of Christ.
- Always grow in the learning of the context and capacities of our hearers, matching the series to the general appetite of the congregation, while expecting their appetites to grow.
- Always seek to evade heaviness and dullness. The revealed truth of God deserves our wonder and excitement! But remember that sometimes the charge of heaviness or dullness requires a consideration of the source. Ask an objective third party.
- Always seek the fullness of the Spirit so that our expositions may be both didactic and empowered.

*Let Us Not*:

- Try to replicate the consecutive expositions of history, even the history of the Lloyd-Jonesian era. Principles are unchanging, contexts are not.
- Think that book-by-book series is the only form of consecutive exposition. While exegesis is fundamental, the series built by it may vary. One may follow a book, another may follow a theme. Writes Stott: ". . . in recommending that the preacher should aim to expound the whole Word of God, I do not mean that he should be clumsy or unimaginative about it."[53]
- Capitulate to contemporary pressures for non-exegetical topical preaching, dogmatically-governed catechetical preaching, or even for a main diet of disconnected texts.
- Conclude the method of consecutive exposition faulty because God uses it initially to sift our churches rather than to fill them.
- Cease to return all glory to God whenever he condescends to use us, whether as a savor of life unto life or death unto death (2 Cor 2:16).

---

[53] Stott, *The Preacher's Portrait*, 23.

*3. The big prayer.*

I share Mr. Murray's focus on the transformation of society through Spirit-filled preaching, but would argue the logical priority of the transformation of the church. After all, is that not where judgment begins (1 Pet 4:17)? Does not the equipping of the saints for the work of ministry come before its fruit, and the revival of the church before the awakening of society? I am not arguing that the church should await the health benefits of exposition before seeking to impact society, but, rather, in Calvinian fashion, that we teach our peers as we learn and learn as we teach, and that we all should go into society as we learn and learn as we go. If we are to be swayed by historical figures at this critical juncture, why not include the gospel work and significant influence of consecutive expositors from the early church fathers as our inspiration, or of the Reformers such as Calvin? Theirs is not an unimpressive track record, and can stand up very well to comparison with the influence which emanated from nineteenth-century Elephant and Castle and twentieth-century Buckingham Gate (although Lloyd-Jones belongs more with the consecutive expositors than Mr. Murray acknowledges).

But whether we focus first on the church or on society, on the likes of Chrysostom and Calvin or Mc'Cheyne and Spurgeon, let us come together to pray for one another, no matter our preferred approach to exposition. Listen to the sense of need in the "voice" of the apostle Paul: ". . . praying at all times in the Spirit, with all prayer and supplication. To that end keep alert with all perseverance, making supplication for all the saints, and also for me, that words may be given to me in opening my mouth boldly to proclaim the mystery of the gospel, for which I am an ambassador in chains, that I may declare it boldly, as I ought to speak" (Eph 6:18–20). Given the pitiful levels of attendance at corporate prayer, we likely need to start training up the youngest converts to make intercession for the ministry of the Word the godly habit of their lifetimes. In Jonathan Edwards's nineteenth and final piece of advice to such, he counsels: "Pray much for the church of God and especially that he would carry on his glorious work that he has now begun. Be much in prayer for ministers of Christ."[54] On that, doubtless all expositors will agree.

---

[54] Jonathan Edwards's Resolutions And Advice to Young Converts, introduced and edited by Stephen J. Nichols (Philipsburg, NJ: P&R Publishing, 2001, 35.

# ABOUT THE AUTHOR

Tim J. R. Trumper (Ph.D., University of Edinburgh) has been Senior Minister of Seventh Reformed Church, Grand Rapids, Michigan, since 2007. His Sunday morning and evening sermons are heard on radio across West Michigan, and are archived at www.7thref.org. Additionally, Dr. Trumper is a monthly panelist on Total Christian Television's internationally broadcast "Ask the Pastor" program. His on-line ministry center is found at www.fromhisfullness.com. He has taught systematic theology, and specializes in the area of soteriology and the doctrine of adoption in particular. He is the author of *When History Teaches Us Nothing: The Recent Reformed Sonship Debate in Context* (Wipf and Stock, 2008), *Preaching and Politics: Engagement without Compromise* (Wipf and Stock, 2009), a number of scholarly articles and chapters, and of the blog series "Adoption Nuggets" (www.togetherforadoption.org). He is a member of the Evangelical Theological Society and the World Reformed Fellowship. Dr. Trumper is married to Brenda. They enjoy worshiping and serving the Lord together, their families, pets, the outdoors, travel, and reading.

www.ingramcontent.com/pod-product-compliance
Lightning Source LLC
Chambersburg PA
CBHW060717030426
42337CB00017B/2903